Your Book of Industrial Archaeology

The Your *Book* Series

Abbeys · Acting · Aeromodelling · Anglo-Saxon England · Animal Drawing · Aquaria · Archaeology · Astronomy · Ballet · Brasses · Breadmaking · Bridges · Butterflies and Moths · Camping · Canals · The Way a Car Works · Card Games · Chess · Corn Dollies · Medieval and Tudor Costume · Nineteenth-Century Costume · Cricket · Dinghy Sailing · Embroidery · English Country Dancing · Film-making · Fishes · Flower Arranging · Flower Making · Forestry · The Guitar · Gymnastics · Hovercraft · Industrial Archaeology · Judo · Kites · Knitted Toys · Knots · Landscape Drawing · Light · Magic · Men in Space · Mental Magic · Modelling · Money · Music · Painting · Paper Folding · Parliament · Party Games · Patchwork · Pet Keeping · Photography · Photographing Wild Life · Keeping Ponies · Prehistoric Animals · Prehistoric Britain · Pressed and Dried Flowers · Puppetry · Racing and Sports Cars · The Recorder · Roman Britain · Sea Fishing · The Seashore · Secret Writing · Self-Defence · Shell Collecting · Skating · Soccer · Swimming · Survival Swimming and Life Saving · Table Tennis · Table Tricks · Tall Ships · Television · Tennis · Traction Engines · Watching Wild Life · Woodwork.

YOUR BOOK OF

Industrial Archaeology

CHRISTINE VIALLS

FABER AND FABER London and Boston

First published in 1981
by Faber and Faber Limited
3 Queen Square London WC1N 3AU
Typeset by King's English Typesetters, Cambridge. Printed by Lowe and Brydone Printers Limited Thetford, Norfolk

British Library Cataloguing in Publication Data
Vialls, Christine
Your book of industrial archaeology.
1. Industrial archaeology – Juvenile literature
I. Title
609 T37

ISBN 0-571-11633-7

Contents

Acknowledgements

Acknowledgements for illustrations are due to:
L. J. Dalby No. 1
The Science Museum Nos. 2, 18
North Wales News Pictures No. 3
Department of the Environment No. 16
United Kingdom Atomic Energy Authority No. 17
Guildhall Library No. 22, 25
The Manchester Ship Canal Company Nos. 30, 31
Wedgwood Public Relations Department No. 32
Minet Library Nos. 36–9
Manchester Public Library No. 43
Macclesfield Public Library No. 47
George Robb RIBA No. 48

Nos. 26 and 27 were drawn by David Vialls.
Nos. 44 – 46 and 49 were provided by pupils of the King's School, Macclesfield
No. 50 was taken by George Vialls (1843–1912).
All other photographs were taken by Arthur Vialls.

Illustrations

The photograph on the back cover is of an old pottery kiln at Coalport, Shropshire

CHAPTER ONE

Noticing: getting interested

What is industrial archaeology? It is the study of buildings and objects connected with industry, in the past – and in the present.

Digging tons of mud from the bottom of an old canal lock – this is the type of job which most people would associate with industrial archaeologists.

Fig. 1 *Volunteers cleaning mud from the derelict Widmead Lock on the Kennet and Avon Canal in 1977*

Fig. 2 *Concorde 002, the first prototype assembled in England, on which many trial flights were made, being moved into a hanger at the Yeovilton museum.*

People visiting the museum at Yeovilton to see Concorde 002 are doing something much less strenuous. Yet this too is industrial archaeology, for they are finding out about a piece of machinery which was once of the greatest importance but now is merely something in a museum. A visit of this kind can start you on a lifetime's interest in industrial archaeology.

Most people are fascinated by transport – whether represented by Concorde or by a canal, by a Roman road or a pack-horse bridge. The transport section of the Science Museum in London probably has more visitors than any other department.

But many people have begun to feel that it is more exciting to try to preserve a whole railway than just to keep parts of it in a museum.

Preservation societies have been formed in many parts of the country to restore and work some of the small railways which would otherwise have been closed. On any day in the holiday season their stations are crowded with visitors looking at the engines or waiting for a ride. They experience something of the past as they feel the hardness of the seats and the vibration of the carriage aboard a steam train, which is itself a living museum of transport. Keeping these lines working is yet another form of industrial archaeology.

A small railway is being used in a different way at the Llechwedd slate mine near Blaenau Ffestiniog. For many years trains were used to carry slate round the quarries. Now the company has built a special line to carry visitors round the works. It would obviously be dangerous to let them wander about on their own, but once they are sitting in the small train they can be carried through the underground quarries, and experience for themselves the feeling of being inside the old workings.

Only people with special training can safely attempt to study the industrial archaeology of mines on their own, but the railway at the Llechwedd slate mine gives amateurs a chance to go underground without any risk.

Fig. 3 *Visitors looking at one of the exhibits as the train carries them throught the Llechwedd Slate Caverns*

Many of the things which interest industrial archaeologists are still in use in towns or in the country. Bridges are a good example, as many still being used were built hundreds of years ago.

Probably few bridges in Britain remained in use as long as the old bridge over the river Exe at Exeter. We know from local records that work started on it in about 1190 and probably took over forty years to complete. The bridge stood until 1778, when a new one was opened. But

Fig.4 *Land arches of the medieval bridge at Exeter which still survive today. They carried modern road traffic as late as the second half of the twentieth century*

it is still possible to see part of the old bridge. As well as the arches over the water, it had a number of land arches. These were similar to the river arches, but were built to carry the road over the marshlands on the north bank, which no doubt flooded regularly in bad weather.

When the second bridge was built in 1778, a new road was made leading from the city to the new bridge and no one thought it necessary to demolish the old land arches. As time went on, buildings were constructed over the arches, and in one place a new road passed over them.

A few years ago buildings were demolished to make way for a new road scheme near the river. Beneath the buildings the old land arches were found still standing – probably looking very much as they did when they were built nearly eight hundred years ago. And most of that time they had carried the weight of traffic – even of modern heavy lorries.

The Exeter City Council have decided to preserve these old arches, and now it is possible to visit them and admire the workmanship of the builders who started work on them only about a hundred years after the death of William the Conqueror.

For the industrial archaeologist this provides a unique opportunity to study the building methods of seven and eight centuries ago, and may help us to date other very old bridges which are perhaps not as well documented as Exe Bridge.

Bridges do not have to be as old as this one to be of interest to industrial archaeologists. At Aberfeldy in Scotland there is a beautiful bridge built as part of a road network by General Wade. After the Scottish uprising of 1715 the English government decided that military roads must be built in Scotland if the army was to be able to control the Highlands. The bridge at Aberfeldy was one of over thirty bridges which the General built. Many of them are still in use. A few have been by-passed during road building operations in recent years, but such is the interest in them that some have been left standing even though they no longer carry traffic.

Fig.5 *Aberfeldy Bridge*

Before the invention of powerful electric and diesel motors, large stationary steam engines were used for a wide variety of work such as driving machinery in mills and workshops, pumping away sewage, lifting water for land drainage.

Fig.6 *Settle Bridge, Yorkshire. It is easy to see that this bridge has been widened. The far section with the stone ribs is almost certainly the oldest section.*

Fig.7 *Crofton Pumping Station on an open day, with Wilton Water in the foreground*

Very few of these engines are still in use, but through the work of preservation societies it is possible for us to experience the heat, steam and smell of a large steam engine house in one of the steam museums which have been set up in various parts of Britain. Crofton Pumping Station is an example.

When the Kennet and Avon Canal was built to form a waterway from the Bristol Channel to London, the engineers had to face the usual problem of how to provide a suitable and constant supply of water for the highest section of the canal. They decided to use Wilton Water, a small lake nearby. However, as Wilton Water was lower than the canal, a pumping station had to be built to lift the water to its summit level. Two large steam pumping engines were installed, and worked until 1958, when an electric pump replaced the steam pumps. The coal needed to keep the engines in steam even when there was little traffic on the waterway was very costly, and the electric pump was cheaper to run.

By 1951 it seemed certain that the whole of the canal would be closed, so a number of people who were interested in preserving it formed themselves into The Kennet and Avon Trust and fought the Minister of Transport to stop the canal being filled in. Not only did they succeed, but they also started to work on it, repairing broken locks, and dredging lengths of canal so that much of it can now be used by holiday-makers.

So successful were they that in 1967 they were able to buy the old pumping station, together with all the equipment. The whole building had to be repaired and a great deal of work was done on the engines themselves. But today they are in working order and during the summer months the Crofton Pumping Station is open for a week-end about once a month so that people can see the great steam pumps lifting the water up into the canal.

Fig.8 *Part of a derelict lock gate on the Kennet and Avon Canal*

CHAPTER TWO

A closer look: finding out more

People who are interested in industrial archaeology are always on the look-out for places and things which are worth visiting. Windmills are an example. They are easy to find, for they are usually built on high ground to catch the wind.

Everybody would recognize the three buildings in the photographs as windmills, but they are quite different in detail. Nutley is a post mill. The whole body of the mill is supported by a post – almost a whole tree – round which the rest of the mill can turn to keep the sails facing into the wind.

Polegate is a tower mill, sturdily built of brick. In a tower mill, only the cap, the very top piece, moves to keep the sails in the eye of the wind.

Shipley is a smock mill – the name given to tower mills made of wood.

These three mills represent the three basic types of windmill. But even between mills of the same type there are differences, because each mill was built by a craftsman who chose his own design. An industrial archaeologist who is interested in windmills will soon begin to notice the little differences between the mills he or she visits – such things as the

Fig.9 *Nutley Post Mill*

Polegate Tower Mill

Shipley Smock Mill

height of the mill, and the shape of the cap. Even the number of sails may differ; not all mills were built with four.

If it is possible to go inside the mills even more differences will be noticed. In some mills the stones will be found to revolve clockwise, but in others they will be going round anti-clockwise. Some millers fitted a bell to warn them when the grain bins were getting empty. Some stones may be only 1 metre in diameter while others may be as large as 2 metres.

Watermills are not so easy to discover, as they are often hidden in remote valleys where mountain streams, running rapidly down steep hillsides, could be used to power the wheels. But an industrial archaeologist soon learns to recognize a watermill even if there is no wheel visible. As with windmills, every watermill is different and the differences may well be much greater, as they were used to turn a great variety of machinery. Many watermills were probably built to mill grain, but may have been altered later so that they could grind things like snuff. Other watermills may have been specially built to turn hundreds of spinning machines in a textile mill.

Cheddleton mill is easy to identify, with its two great wheels out in the open. It is now a museum where we can study the old process of flint-crushing and see all the machinery still working. Cheddleton is not far from Stoke-on-Trent, the area we call the Potteries, and the crushed flint the mill produced was for making pottery.

Fig.10 *Cheddleton Watermill, Staffordshire*

Fig. 11 *Higherford Toll House, Lancashire*

Industrial archaeologists travelling round Britain can often find toll houses by the side of the road. These cottages were probably built between about 1700 and 1830.

In the seventeenth century roads were in a bad state of repair, and in 1663 some wealthy men in East Anglia told Parliament that they would repair some of the local roads if they were allowed to collect a toll from everyone who used them. Acts of Parliament were passed and the system worked so well that during the next hundred years roads all over Britain were repaired in this way by groups of people who formed themselves into companies called Turnpike Trusts. Gates called turnpikes were built across the roads and travellers had to pay before the gate could be opened for them. As tolls had to be collected both day and night, cottages were built beside the roads for the toll keepers and their families to live in.

Fig. 12 *Stanton Drew Toll House, Somerset*

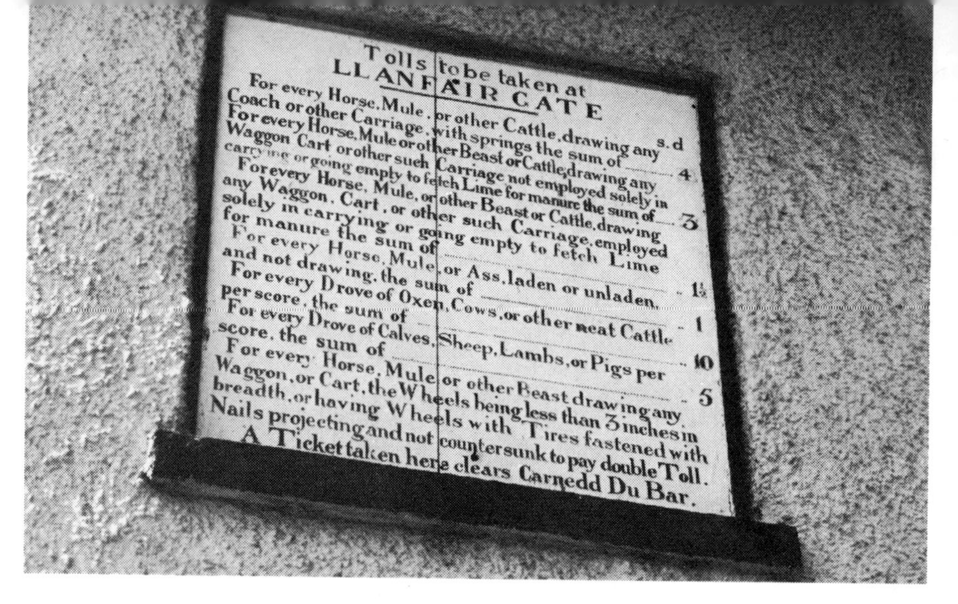

Fig. 13 *List of toll charges at the Llanfair Toll House, Anglesey*

If we look at the old lists of toll charges they give us a very good idea of the kind of traffic that passed the gate. Businessmen and rich people probably travelled by coach. Carts often carried goods to market but might be fetching lime. Lime was spread on the land as a fertilizer, particularly on peaty soil, and helped to produce better crops, so a cart carrying lime had to pay only half the normal toll. Pack-horses were obviously still common, as there was a special charge for them. Cows and other animals were driven to market along the roads and tolls had to be paid for them.

Many of the Acts of Parliament allowing roads to be turnpiked made it a condition that the Trust should erect mileposts along the roads and put up signposts at crossroads. Many of these were made of cast iron.

Fig. 14 *Mileposts:*
Bowbells: 36 miles from the church of St. Mary-le-Bow in the City of London
Keighley and Kendal Road

Fig. 15 *Even though people now live in this oast house, there can be no doubt about its original purpose*

Many coaching inns probably date from the turnpike age. Even though travel was much faster on the new improved roads it still took four and a half days to travel from Manchester to London in 1754, which meant several nights spent on the road. Industrial archaeologists can usually spot the old coaching inns because of the archway under which the coach would pass to reach the courtyard behind. The passengers would board the coach in the courtyard; the richer people rode inside, while the poorer travelled on top. As the coach left the inn, the outside passengers would have had to bend low as it passed under the archway into the road.

CHAPTER THREE

Life before the machine age

Some people think that industrial archaeology covers only the years from about 1750 to 1850. This is the time which we call the Industrial Revolution, when Britain changed from a country where most things were made by hand to one where people depend on machines. But we have already found that Concorde 002 and many other equally modern things are now in museums. It is also true that industrial archaeologists study many things which were in use before 1750, such as watermills, which were used by the Romans nearly 2000 years ago. So how far back must the industrial archaeologist go?

If we define an industry as the making of something, not just for our own use, but for sale, then probably the oldest industrial site in Britain is in Norfolk, at a place called Grimes Graves. There, Stone Age people dug between 700 and 800 circular pits to reach the good-quality flints they needed to make axe-heads. Judging by the size and number of these pits, far more axe-heads must have been made than could possibly have been used by the local community. It seems certain that the makers must have been selling or bartering axe-heads for other things.

Fig. 16 *An artist's impression of Grimes Graves*

Fig. 17 *The experimental Fast Reactor at Dounreay was closed down in March 1977. It is now industrial archaeology.*

We even have proof that this was so. Geologists who have made a special study of the types of flint found in different parts of Britain have examined flint tools found by archaeologists digging Stone Age sites. Because flint from each area has slightly different characteristics these geologists have been able to say with certainty that axes made at Grimes Graves were being used by New Stone Age people in places as far away as Dorset.

So industrial archaeology can cover agricultural machinery, sources of power such as waterwheels, electricity generation plant, coal mines or a Stone Age flint mine. It takes in the work of the blacksmith who uses his muscles and his skill to work things from iron, and the modern factory where steel is shaped by a giant press. The industrial archaeologist is interested in a man making rope by hand, and the evolution of the bicycle from the "hobby horse" to the racing bikes of today.

But despite this it is true to say that most industrial archaeology is the study of the developments which took place during the Industrial Revolution. This was a period of great changes, but many of them were never described in writing, so we can find out about them only by studying what is left, before it too gets swept away by new road schemes or re-building.

Fig. 18 *'Pedestrian hobby horse'*

Life before 1700

To understand the importance of the Industrial Revolution we need to know a little of what life was like earlier. There were very few towns, and the few there were would seem very small to us today. London was the only large city; Manchester was a small town. One has to remember that

the population of Britain was about 7 million in 1700 instead of today's 54 million.

The majority of people lived in the country in small village communities, the men working on the land, or as thatchers, carpenters, blacksmiths, or at some other country craft.

Each family probably kept a pig or possibly a sheep, which they fattened and killed to give them a supply of pork, bacon and lard, or mutton and wool. Some also had strips of land in the village common fields, on which they grew wheat. This was ground into flour by the local miller, and, from this flour, the women of the family made bread dough, which was baked in the village oven along with the bread for most of the rest of the village.

A family with a larger cottage might have an oven of their own, built into the thick wall beside the fireplace. This would be a stone- or brick-lined cavity. When it was used the whole oven was filled with sticks which were then fired. Once all the wood was burnt, the housewife scraped out the ashes and then put the bread dough or the meat into the hot oven and closed the door. The bricks or stones of the oven kept hot long enough for the food to cook through. These ovens can still be found in some old cottages.

The most important material for the villagers was wood. The frames of their cottages were made of it, and unless they lived in a coal-mining area, they burned wood to keep themselves warm and to cook their food. They had very little metal in their cottages. A copper cooking pot to hang over the open fire was so precious that it would be mentioned specially in the owner's will.

Fig. 19 *A timber-framed house being restored*

What clothes they had were woven from coarse sheep's wool which they spun themselves, and which was then woven for them by the local weaver. Many industrial archaeologists are interested in how cloth was made. A number of museums in different parts of Britain have been set up to show how a weaver worked at his loom. At the Colne Valley Museum in the south of Yorkshire it is possible to visit an old weaver's cottage and to see cloth being made very much as it was made two hundred and fifty years ago.

Clothes were made to last, and "my wearing apparel" was mentioned in many wills. Even when a dress or coat was worn out it was not thrown away but was cut down to make clothes for a child. Finally it would end its days as part of a patchwork quilt – a warm covering for a bed.

Wood was as important outside the home as inside. Carts and boats, tools and waterwheels were made from it. The village carpenter could make anything from furniture to the framework of a plough. There might be a cartwright to make the carts and waggons used by the farmers, and a wheelwright to make and mend wheels. There was sure to be a blacksmith who would shoe the horses and make tools such as scythes and shears out of iron.

The only forms of energy available were horse power, wind and water power, and, of course, man power. Windmills were useful until the wind dropped, and watermills as long as water was available. But even a large river could dry up in a time of drought. By making a mill pond it was possible to store energy in the form of water during wet weather, but no mill pond was large enough to store the water needed during a long dry period. Before it could expand, industry needed a much more reliable source of power.

Fig. 20 *Two old weavers' cottages which are now part of the Colne Valley Museum at Golcar, Yorkshire*

Fig. 21 *A demonstration of weaving at the Colne Valley Museum*

Fig.22 *This drawing by W. H. Pyne, published in 1806, shows pack-horses carrying boxes of limestone.*

Fig.23 *Eastergate Bridge, Marsden, Yorkshire. There are still a number of these pack-horse bridges to be found in the hills. Notice the parapets. The width of the packs made it impossible for the pack-horses to cross a narrow bridge unless the parapets were very low, so that the packs could stick out above them.*

Most goods were carried by water or on horseback, in heavy packs slung across the animals' backs. Long strings of these pack-horses were formed, the reins of one horse being plaited into the tail of the horse in front, so that one or two men could lead a train of perhaps forty horses along the pack-horse routes. These tracks were often narrow and steep, climbing from one valley to the next over the top of the hills – the shortest route – no matter how hard it was for the men or the horses. On these narrow mountain passes the leading horse often carried a bell which would ring as he walked, the sound of the bell warning the men in charge of a pack-horse train coming the other way to wait at a suitable passing place until the first train of horses had gone by.

Fig.24 *Part of the stone trackway of an old pack-horse route. Many can still be found in different parts of Britain, particularly in hilly country.*

Fig.25 *A heavy stage waggon, from a book of drawings by W. H. Pyne, published in 1806.*

Anything which could not be carried by pack-horse had to travel in one of the heavy waggons pulled by as many as eight or ten horses. These travelled very slowly, probably at no more than walking pace. Their heavy loads caused the wheels to cut up the surface of the muddy roads so that they soon became impassable in bad weather.

CHAPTER FOUR

How life changed in the machine age

By 1700 timber was becoming extremely scarce, for whole forests had been cut down to build ships, especially for the Navy. As we have seen, wood was needed for many different purposes, and one of the biggest uses was in the iron industry. Wood was used to produce the charcoal which was essential for the manufacture of good workable iron.

Ironmasters tried to use coal instead of charcoal in the smelting of iron ore, but they found that sulphur from the coal combined with the iron to make it brittle and useless.

In the early years of the eighteenth century Abraham Darby began to experiment with coke as fuel at his blast furnace at Coalbrookdale in Shropshire. Coke was made by firing large piles of coal and leaving them to smoulder for several days to allow the unwanted gases to burn away, and Darby saw that this was very similar to the making of charcoal from wood.

After some experimenting, he managed to make usable iron in his furnace, using coke instead of charcoal. This iron was suitable for use as cast iron, to be melted and poured into shaped moulds. But it was not good enough for blacksmiths to use. Nevertheless, his discovery was of the greatest importance. At first other ironmasters found it difficult to use his method, but by about 1750 many were using coke in their blast furnaces. At last the iron industry was no longer dependent on the supply of charcoal, and furnaces no longer had to close down regularly because of shortage of fuel.

Another industry which was in difficulties at the start of the eighteenth century was mining. Coal was urgently needed to replace wood as fuel both for domestic fires and for industry, but by 1700 most of the seams which were near the surface had been worked out. As mine owners drove shafts deeper into the earth, they had an increasing problem with flooding. Many coal mines had to close because the pumps available at that time were not powerful enough to keep the workings free from water, and the tin mines in Cornwall suffered from the same problem.

One man who must have been very much aware of the difficulties of the miners was an ironmonger and metal worker from Dartmouth in Devon. His name was Thomas Newcomen. We don't know a great deal about his early life but we think that he travelled round the West Country selling tools to farmers and miners, and possibly making spare parts for the horse-driven pumps used in the mines. In 1712 he built the first really successful steam mine pumping engine in the world. He was not the first man to experiment with steam power, but no one before him had managed to build a pump which would lift enough water to drain a mine.

The Newcomen pumping engine was so successful that within a very few years steam pumping engines were being used in mining areas all over Britain, and even in Europe one was built in the region which is now Czechoslovakia as early as 1722.

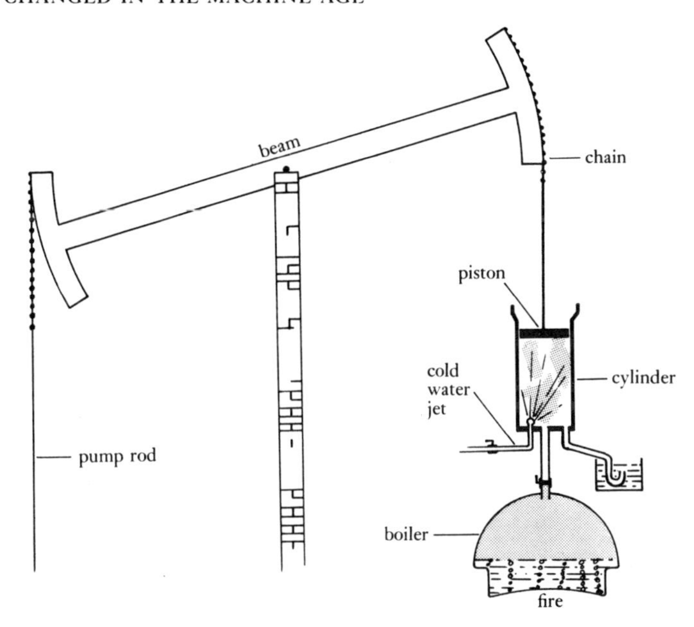

Fig.26 *Newcomen engine. Steam from the boiler filled the cylinder below the raised piston. A jet of cold water, introduced into the cylinder, turned the steam back to water, so making a vaccum below the piston. Air pressure acting on the top of the piston pushed it down to the bottom of the cylinder. As the beam rocked, it lifted the pump rods with their load of water.*

About fifty years after Newcomen built his first successful engine, James Watt, a scientific instrument maker from Glasgow, made certain improvements to the Newcomen-type engine. The cylinder of the Newcomen engine had to be heated and then cooled again each time the engine made a stroke – each time the pump rods lifted. The engine worked slowly because of the time needed to heat the cylinder again. By dividing the heating and cooling functions between two separate cylinders (the second of which he called the condenser) Watt cut the time between each stroke and so not only made a steam pump which worked more quickly but also managed to save on the amount of fuel which was needed.

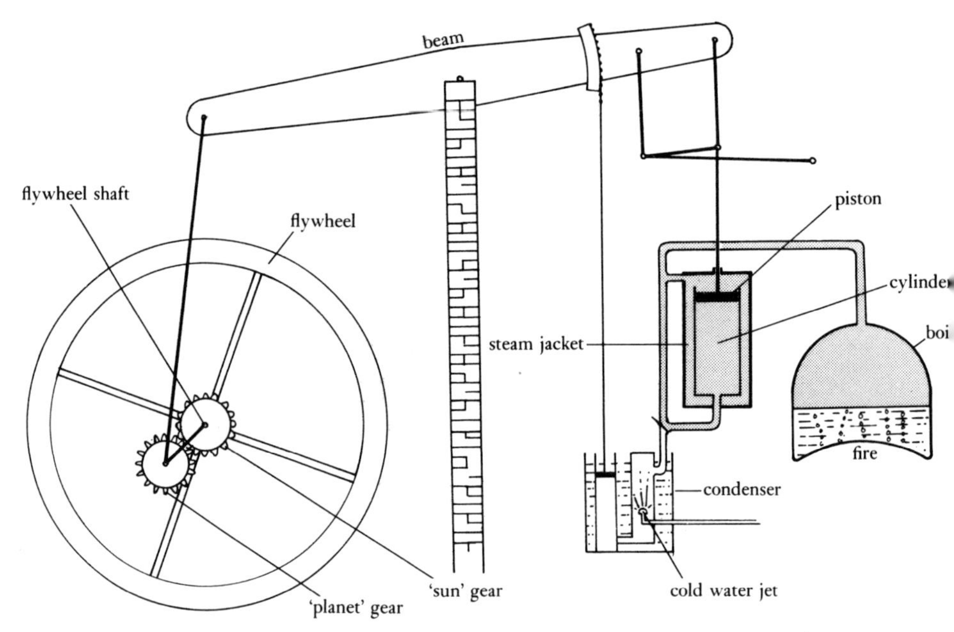

Fig. 27 *Rotative engine, showing how the up and down motion of the beam was changed into a rotative motion to turn the flywheel shaft from which the drive to the machinery was taken.*

In the Watt engine the steam was condensed back into the water in the condenser, so letting the cylinder remain hot all the time. The steam in the steam jacket not only helped to keep the cylinder hot, but also supplied the pressure to push the piston down as the vacuum was formed. As the beam rocked, the 'planet' gear was driven round the 'sun', so turning the flywheel shaft. The heavy flywheel helped to keep the shaft turning smoothly.

The Rotative Engine

In perfecting a really efficient steam pumping engine, Thomas Newcomen and James Watt had helped the mine owners to get rid of unwanted water. But the steam pump was also used to conserve water. Manufacturers who used water power to turn their machinery were often forced to close their works during dry weather, when the flow of the river was insufficient to turn the waterwheels. Even when the wheel was supplied by a mill pond, a long period of drought could use up all the stored water.

But a steam engine could be used to pump the water, which had already turned the wheel, back into the mill pond. In this way, the water could be used over and over again instead of being allowed to run away downstream.

Although this use of the steam pump was very helpful, many manufacturers realized that it would be much more convenient if they could connect their steam engine direct to their machinery. But the basic steam engine could only make things move up and down. What was really needed was a rotative engine – one which was able to turn a wheel. Different ways of doing this were tried, including the 'Sun and Planet' gears designed by James Watt, which are shown in Fig. 27.

Once steam engines had been adapted to work factory machines, which happened in the 1780s, factories were freed from the need for water power. Mill owners no longer had to build their manufactories high in the hills beside swift-running streams. The sluggish rivers of the valley bottom could produce all the water they needed to cool the condensers of their Watt engines: very soon the lower valleys of the north of England were filled with mills, as large industrial towns grew up, concentrating on the making of textiles.

New Uses for Iron

Once iron had become easily available, many new uses were found for it, such as the mileposts mentioned in Chapter 2.

Fig.28 *Iron bridge in the Close, Exeter. After the opening of the great Iron Bridge in the Severn Gorge, Shropshire, in 1781, many engineers began to use iron for bridge building. This small bridge looks like a miniature of the great bridge over the River Severn.*

Fig.29 *Strutt's Mill at Belper in Derbyshire, one of the earliest manufactories made with an iron frame. Here you can see the slim iron pillars which hold up the iron beams of the floor above.*

One of the most important uses in its effect on daily life was probably the making of iron-framed buildings. There had been many disastrous fires in the large mills which had been built in the second half of the eighteenth century. The grease from the machinery would soak into the wooden floors of the building. If a fire started, perhaps caused by a spark from one of the machines, it would spread with alarming speed through the oily timber.

New factories were built with iron pillars and iron beams holding up brick arches. The floors above the arches were often covered with tiles rather than wood. Buildings of this type could still burn, but were less likely to catch fire. If a fire did start, the mill workers had a better chance of escaping, and much less damage would be done.

As well as the mills themselves, many of the machines used in them came to be made of iron instead of wood.

CHAPTER FIVE

The transport revolution

Canals

Better methods of moving goods had to be found before industry could expand. The easiest form of transport had always been by water, but many areas of Britain were a long way from a navigable river. In the seventeenth century many rivers were dredged, sharp bends were straightened and weirs were built to deepen the upper reaches. This enabled boats to travel further inland and brought river transport within easy reach of many more parts of the country.

Despite this, many goods had to finish their journey by cart or pack-horse. This was very slow, as they had to be unshipped and re-loaded, and vast numbers of horses were needed.

In the middle of the eighteenth century, the Duke of Bridgewater decided to build a canal from his coal mines at Worsley to Manchester, a few miles away. To reach Manchester the canal had to cross the river Irwell and the Duke and his advisers built a stone aqueduct to carry the canal over it. Because no one in Britain had ever built anything like that before, it caused great interest and crowds travelled from miles round to see the boats sailing over what looked like an ordinary bridge across the river.

The Bridgewater canal also caused a great deal of interest for quite a different reason. The price of coal from the Worsley mines was halved once the canal was finished, as transporting it by water was so much easier than carrying it by pack-horse.

Fig.30 *The famous Barton aqueduct on the Bridgewater Canal, photographed shortly before it was demolished. When it was opened in 1761 people travelled from miles round to see the boats sailing over what looked like an ordinary bridge.*

Fig. 31 *When the Manchester ship canal was built, the famous old Barton aqueduct was demolished and replaced by the present swing aqueduct. In this aerial photograph the aqueduct and the road bridge are both open to allow a ship to pass along the canal.*

Businessmen were quick to see the advantages of building canals. Josiah Wedgwood, the founder of the famous pottery firm, realized that things such as cups, plates and teapots were much less likely to get broken if transported by barge than by pack-horse. It would also be easier for him to get supplies of clay and other materials he needed if he had a canal close to his factory. He convinced other businessmen of the advantages of canal building and they agreed to join him in building a network of canals all over the Midlands and the North. By 1800 hundreds of miles of canal had been built, linking London, Bristol, the river Mersey and the river Humber.

Fig. 32 *Part of the factory which Josiah Wedgwood built beside the Trent and Mersey Canal*

Fig. 33 *It is still possible to find remains of the old Stockton and Darlington Railway like these stone sleepers to which the original track was fastened*

Railways

The building of the canals made a vast difference to trade in Britain, but barges could travel only at the rate of the horses which pulled them. Merchants began to wish for quicker forms of transport.

From about 1600 some mine owners had been using wooden waggonways for moving coal and other heavy goods over short distances from the quarries and mines to the river banks. These waggonways, like our modern railways, used flanged wheels which ran on raised wooden or iron rails. Most of these waggonways were built on a long gradual slope from the quarries on high ground down to the river level. The trucks ran down under their own weight. After they were emptied into the waiting boats, the empty trucks were pulled back up the slope by horses.

In the first few years of the nineteenth century, a number of men began to experiment with steam locomotives for use on these waggonways. One of them was George Stephenson, who built twelve steam locomotives for the mining company for which he worked and soon gained a reputation as an engineer. When businessmen in the North East decided to build a waggonway from some mines near Darlington to the docks at Stockton, they asked George Stephenson to help them.

Because he believed in steam locomotives, he suggested that they should use steam power instead of horses. Eventually it was agreed to employ steam power to pull coal waggons, but it was felt that it would be too dangerous to use it to pull passenger coaches.

In 1823, two years before the Stockton and Darlington Railway was opened, other men from South Lancashire visited the North East to see George Stephenson and to find out about the new railway line. They were so much impressed by what they saw that they asked Stephenson to build a railway for them from Liverpool to Manchester.

In an effort to find the best locomotive for their line, the directors of the Liverpool Manchester Railway offered a prize of £500 – a great deal of money in those days. At Rainhill, near Liverpool, four steam locomotives were tested. The winner was *Rocket*, built by George Stephenson's son Robert. Although it did much better than the other engines, the company also bought two of the other locomotives, and so their line became the first railway in the world to run a regular passenger service pulled by steam locomotives.

Fig. 34 *From an early postcard of the Liverpool and Manchester Railway. Notice that the coach looks just like three road coaches mounted on railway truck wheels.*

Fig.35 *Most old Roman roads are probably buried deep underneath some of our modern roads, but Blackstone Edge is steep and crosses high moorland, and so has probably never been used by wheeled traffic since the Romans left Britain.*

As had happened with the Duke of Bridgewater's canal, the building of the Liverpool Manchester Railway caused great interest throughout Britain. Within ten years trains were able to travel at between thirty and forty miles an hour, a very much faster means of travel, and of moving goods, than either the canals or the road transport of those days. Thousands of miles of railway were built. In a very few years the old coach roads were deserted except for local traffic, and the canals began to lose more and more of their trade to the faster "iron road".

In the twentieth century it has become the turn of the railways to lose business to the heavy road lorry. Just as many miles of canal were abandoned or filled in, so hundreds of miles of railway line have been closed and the rails taken up and sold for scrap.

Industrial archaeologists have many strands of transport history to study. On Blackstone Edge near Rochdale they can see a Roman road looking very much as it did when it was built. Pack-horse routes can be found winding their way over mountain passes. In the valleys, modern road traffic rushes past the occasional toll house, or crosses a canal bridge, the drivers perhaps being unaware of the water below.

Some of the closed railway lines have been turned into public footpaths and the rambler can walk across old viaducts which used to carry steam trains. In other places all that is left is a deserted track on which the industrial archaeologist may find a derelict station platform, or an old signal, or one of the long pins which once held the shining metal track to the wooden sleepers.

CHAPTER SIX

Working on Projects

Once we have started to notice industrial monuments as we travel round the towns or the countryside, we naturally become curious and feel a desire to find out more about them.

A group from a school in south-east London decided to try to find out what industries there were in the area around the school. Perhaps what surprised them most was to find a blacksmith working, making things like wrought-iron gates for houses. The firm for which he worked also had an engineering works with welding equipment, drilling machines, lathes, etc. When the group from the school spoke to the lady who runs the firm, she told them that her father had been a blacksmith and farrier and that when he died she and her mother decided to run the firm themselves.

She also told them about the old smithy building a few hundred yards away, which her father had used when he first started and which had probably been a blacksmith's forge for many, many years.

The group found that the old smithy was one of a set of industrial buildings grouped round an open space called Woodman's Yard, which included a garage, a laundry and a printer's. The forge building was completely derelict, the roof having fallen in. All they could see to show that it had once been used by a blacksmith was the chimney of the forge, which was still standing.

The blacksmith working near the school did not shoe horses, but the group realized that there must be farriers working in London, shoeing the police horses, the large dray horses which some breweries still use to deliver casks of beer, and the horses of the rag-and-bone men who still work in parts of London, asking for rubbish from door to door.

By looking at old street directories in the local record office they found out more about the area. There had been an hotel called the Woodman on the main road just beside the entrance to Woodman's Yard, and a directory of 1838 stated that coaches ran from there to the centre of London about six miles away.

A map dated about 1864 marked the Woodman and showed the yard as the Hotel Stables, but a street directory dated 1882, after listing the hotel, showed a livery stables, a firm of jobbing masters who hired out small horse-drawn vehicles, a wheelwright, a shoeing forge, and a laundry. From this it looked as if the old hotel stables had been taken over by several small firms. Perhaps the coaching firms later turned into garages, while the blacksmith's business is now mainly an engineering concern.

The group found that there had been a blacksmith in Woodman's Yard since 1838; perhaps if they had gone back through older records they would have found that one had been working there even earlier. There are still many questions to answer. When was the Woodman built? When did coaches stop running from there to London? Has there been a laundry in Woodman's Yard ever since 1882?

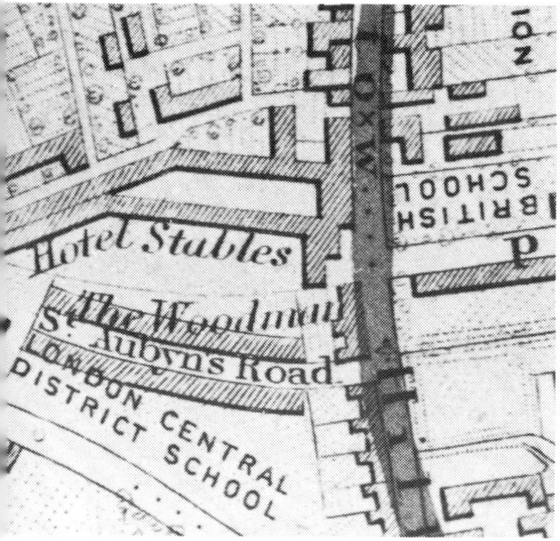

Fig. 36 *This map drawn in about 1864 shows the Woodman Hotel and the stables behind it, which were later to become the industrial complex known as Woodman's Yard.*

Fig. 37 *An old picture of the Woodman Hotel*

Fig. 38 *This street directory gave a list of the coaches which went to London from the Woodman and Spa Hotel in 1838*

Coaches,

From Norwood to London.

Mosley & Glovers coaches from *Woodman & Spa Hotel* to London, morn. 8, ½ p. 8, 9, ½ p. 9; aft. ½ p. 2, ¼ bef. 6, ½ p. 6, ½ p. 7.

Fig. 39 *A page from a street directory, dated 1882, showing the Woodman Hotel and the firms which must have been occupying the old stables*

Royal Terrace.

1 Stafford F., bootmaker
2 Clarke T., cheesemngr.
3 Jobbins H. T., cnfctnr.
4 Ward & Sons, butchers
NUNNERLEY BROS., fancy drapers
The Woodman, Mrs. M. Wilson
Jeffery Mrs., livery stable keeper
Cook & Coppin, job-masters
Phillips J., whlwright.
Bradford T., laundry
Murrell I., shng. forge

The Mineral Railway Track

Two people walking along a valley in Snowdonia found their path crossed by a set of small gauge railway lines, and asked the farmer for permission to leave the path and follow the railway to see why it had been built. They walked towards the hills at the top of the valley and eventually found that the tracks led to a slate quarry. After satisfying themselves that this was the reason for the building of the railway, they retraced their steps and then followed the tracks down the valley.

This proved to be a much more interesting walk. The land fell away sharply, and because of this the builders of the railway had had to carry the line down very steeply in places. These sections, known as inclined planes, were much too steep for trucks to run down without some form of brake. A length of steel rope lying down the middle of the inclined plane showed that the trucks must have been attached to this before being lowered down – probably by some sort of engine which allowed the cable to unwind from a drum at the top of the slope.

At the top of the first inclined plane the walkers could see no signs of a building which might have housed a steam winding engine, but lower down the valley they came across a house standing exactly on the track. It was only when they had passed the house and looked back at it from below that they saw, from its shape, that it must originally have been the winding house through which the trucks actually passed on their way down the inclined plane.

Fig.40 *The high section of this house, which lies right on the track of the old railway, was almost certainly the winding house for lowering and raising the trucks*

Fig.41 *Old truck wheels lying beside the track of the old Croesor railway*

The two walkers found many things of interest on their journey down the valley – a set of points, couplings from some old waggons and a set of wheels lying beside the track, and several small bridges which had carried the railway over mountain streams.

Later, in a shop, they found a booklet describing some of the small railways in that part of Snowdonia. They learned that their track had been built in 1863, and many other details about the history of the railway in which they had become interested.

Hand Block Printing

After being shown a textile printing block one industrial archaeologist decided to read a book on the subject, only to find that there was practically no printed information on how the blocks were made. This led to an intensive research project lasting several years.

Fig.42 *Part of the printing surface of an old block used for printing patterns on silk material*

Old craftsmen were visited, tools examined and techniques documented. An old piece of machinery was found to have a patent number, so long hours were spent in the Patent Office in London looking at the drawings of the machine and finding out who had invented it. Eventually all the findings of this researcher were published and an old craft was documented before it was too late.

The Bridge that Fell Down

The great engineer Isambard Kingdom Brunel pasted a newspaper cutting into his diary about Broughton Suspension Bridge, which collapsed in 1831 as a detachment of soldiers was marching over it. This cutting led an industrial archaeologist to search through old newspapers, until a complete account of the incident was built up. A reference in the *Manchester Guardian* to a highly technical article in the publications of a learned society led to the finding of a diagram of the bridge and eventually to an actual photograph taken of the rebuilt bridge just before it was finally demolished (see p. 56).

All these projects have two distinct threads. Firstly there is the examination of an actual site or tool or machine: the exploration of the school's own area, the inspection of the bridge remains, interviewing old craftsmen and looking at the blocks they made.

The other thread is that of research in books and documents. Without that the two walkers would never have known when their railway was built, and of course the man who wrote the book which they bought had gone back to original documents and deeds himself – he too was an industrial archaeologist.

Fig. 43 *Broughton Suspension Bridge*

The researcher looking into the making of textile printing blocks consulted rare books at the British Library, old patent specifications at the Patent Office, census returns and street directories in the local history section of the public library. The bridge that collapsed was documented in old newspapers of the time. These and many other sources can be used by the industrial archaeologist in his or her search for information.

CHAPTER SEVEN

The garret houses project

A project on Macclesfield Weavers' Houses, researched and written by a group from the King's School, Macclesfield. All the photographs in the project were taken by one of the group and all the other illustrations were drawn or collected as part of the project.

Garret Houses

The manufacture of silk has been an integral part of the history of Macclesfield for over two hundred years, and yet is now almost non-existent. The past fifty years have seen a steady decline in the relative importance of silk weaving, and it has become apparent that some record must be made of this traditional industry before its total extinction.

During the sixteenth century Huguenot refugees from religious persecution in France settled in London and founded the silk-weaving industry. It was already well established in England by 1700 and before half of the next century had passed, Macclesfield was celebrated for its manufacture of buttons of silk and mohair wrought with the needle and worn on fully trimmed suits.

The Napoleonic Wars 1793/1815 was a period of great prosperity for Macclesfield – the blockading of French ports by British ships gave the town's silk trade an enormous boost.

The work of the hand loom weaver was generally carried out in the attic or "garret" of his own house – a large room on the third floor characterized by its long low windows, access to which was gained either through the house or by an external staircase. Recently Macclesfield has seen large scale changes to parts of the town either by modernization or demolition of the garret houses. It was this which led us to feel a need for a record of the town's near unique past. As far as we know no one has ever attempted to make a record of garrets in this manner and so we were on new territory with no precedents to refer to and no detailed framework of what we were looking for.

The first problem that we encountered was locating all the garret houses. It is thought that there was a map showing the position of the garret houses in the possession of the Macclesfield Borough Council, but unfortunately we were unable to obtain access to this. The group decided collectively to start with the maps of the town provided by a local estate agent. With the aid of these simple guides to the layout of the town centre, we then divided into several groups, each with an area to survey for garret houses.

This proved not quite as simple as one might expect, as some of these garret homes had been modernized or altered in some way. It is not sufficient to list most three-storey terraces, because there was considerable confusion between garret houses and three-storey shops of a similar age which, though smaller, are difficult to differentiate from the exterior. Not all garret houses showed the typical type of window peculiar to houses of this type. One building measured in Great King Street was discovered to be a shop when the interior was inspected.

The group then returned to the school to compile information upon the map. Most of the garrets were found to be single although there was evidence in some cases that they had previously connected to two or more other properties. We even found one excellent example of a garret spanning five houses which were unmodernized in Daintry Street off Buxton Road.

Fig.44 *A typical garret window*

Once all the house numbers and street names were gathered and placed on the map we were able to form an idea of just how many there were. In Macclesfield's case there were several hundred garrets and these were, as expected, sited within close proximity to the town centre, within one kilometre in most cases.

It was then decided which of the garret houses would be the most interesting for an internal survey. This we determined by the ease of access and quality of the original buildings. Access we found to be the main contributory factor in the decisions because it was agreed that those which were occupied had a very much greater likelihood of being modernized or altered in some way.

However, most of those properties relevant to our project, which were being sold by estate agents in the town, were empty and completely unmodernized. One must mention at this point the most generous co-operation of these estate agents who supplied our group with literature on specific properties as well as keys for inspections and in one case even a copy of a set of deeds.

The number of garrets available for survey proved quite sufficient for our particular needs. The great majority of the garrets built during the nineteenth century are still erect today. In fact it is common belief that these houses are of more sound construction than more contemporary structures within the town. After all, these garrets were built in large blocks which were to house not only families but machines too, and furthermore, the greater part of them were built for rent and so had a higher standard of fittings than other houses in the town.

The houses inhabited by the Macclesfield hand loom weavers were very similar in construction. On the whole they were made up of five rooms. A typical house would have three on the ground floor, made up of a front sitting room about 13′ 6″ × 12′ 5″ (4.05 × 3.72 m.), a living room about 13′ 4″ × 12′ 3″ (4 × 3.69 m.) and a small cramped kitchen about 8′ 3″ × 6′ 3″ (2.47 × 1.87 m.). On the first floor there were two bedrooms, the first being 13′ 3″ × 12′ 5″ (3.97 × 3.72 m.) and the rear being 13′ 3″ × 12′ 7″ (3.97 × 3.77 m.). They would be joined to the ground floor by a steep narrow stair with a right-angle turn at the base.

The stairs to the garret would be much steeper and narrower and lead through a trap door into the garret itself. In some garrets access was via a spiral staircase as in Daintry Terrace where the garret runs the whole length of the row of houses.

The garrets were lofty and airy, about 27′ 4″ × 12′ 5″ (9.20 × 3.77 m.), the roof rising to a point about 10′ (3 m.) above the floor. The windows, which extended for almost the whole width of the room, are never very high, about 2′ 6″ (.76 m.) with leaded panes. On one wall of each garret we always found a blocked up door between chimney breasts. This suggests they were built in pairs with one man owning both or renting out one of the houses or his garret.

Garrets were not always used for the purpose for which they were built, so after measuring the garrets we looked for physical evidence of any weaving that had taken place there, on the beams and windowsills and even under the floorboards. It was while searching under the floorboards that some faded silk threads were found, and interesting features observed were photographed.

We found evidence of silk weaving in other garrets too – there were porcelain rings hanging from beams in the roof, inside which coloured threads were placed while setting up the looms. There were also curious

Fig.45 *As no records of the dimensions of a garret house could be found, it was felt that one of the essential parts of the project was to measure and record, in the form of scale drawings, a typical garret house. Here you see four of a set made of a house in St. George Street, Macclesfield. The measurements are given in feet and inches, which was the system in use when the houses were built.*

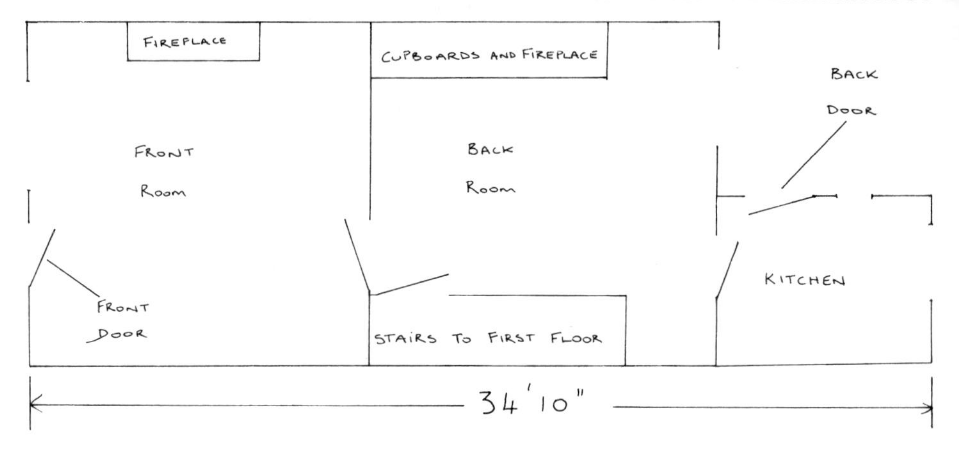

PLAN OF GROUND FLOOR

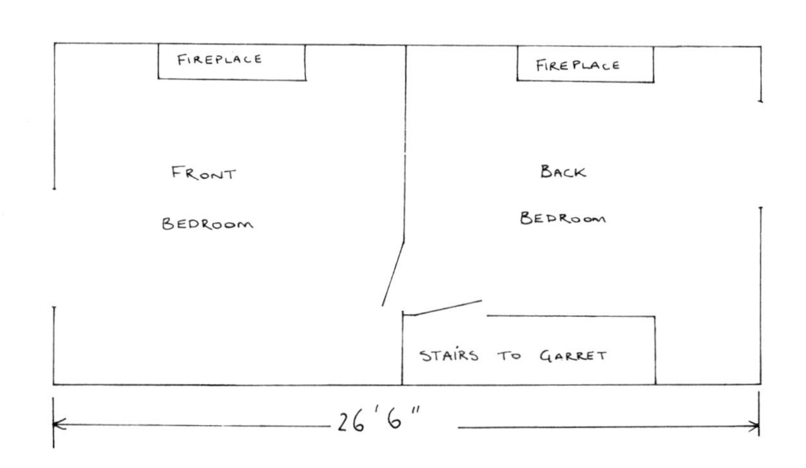

PLAN OF BEDROOMS ON FIRST FLOOR

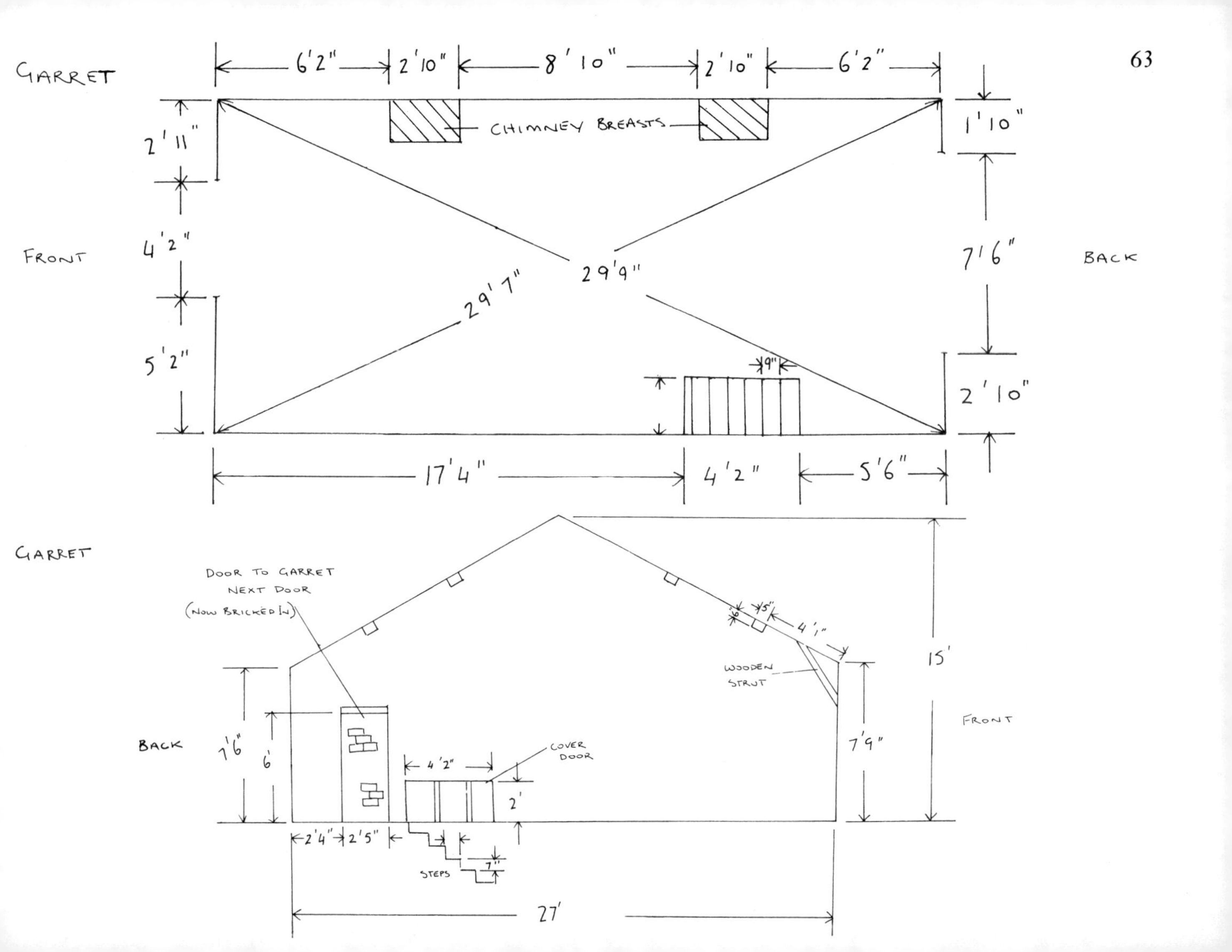
GARRET
6'2"
2'10"
8'10"
2'10"
6'2"
CHIMNEY BREASTS
2'11"
1'10"
FRONT
4'2"
29'9"
7'6"
BACK
29'7"
5'2"
9"
2'10"
17'4"
4'2"
5'6"
GARRET
DOOR TO GARRET
NEXT DOOR
(NOW BRICKED IN)
6"
5"
4'1"
WOODEN
STRUT
15'
FRONT
BACK
7'6"
6'
4'2"
COVER
DOOR
7'9"
2'
2'4"
2'5"
7"
STEPS
27'

Fig.46 *One of the boys measuring the window in a garret*

spikes and holes in the garrets we visited which may have been used by the weavers in their occupation.

None of the local historians knew the date of construction of these buildings and we felt that their age was an essential part of the overall picture. The first way that came to mind, and the surest, was to examine the deeds. However it was often impossible to find the relevant deeds as many prior to 1900 have been destroyed. Finally we succeeded in obtaining photocopies of a set of deeds, relating to part of Paradise Street, through the help of a local estate agent which established a definite date of buildings as being 1826–27.

However the difficulty in obtaining deeds forced us to use less exact methods. St. George's Street was dated by establishing the date of construction of the church at the end of the street as being 1822, when it was built as a chapel to accommodate seventeen hundred Dissenters. We can therefore plausibly assume that this community was established immediately prior to 1822, and census records show us exceptional increases in the population of this area during the 1820s – greater than in either the previous or following decades.

The 1825 Directory revealed the presence of weavers "Who have looms at their own houses" in St. George's Street. This confirms the date of construction as being definitely before 1825. Census returns also proved the age of Daintry Terrace to be of a similar period. These census returns were found on microfilm in the local history sections of the town library, where they are easily accessible to the general public after a century as they are on a one hundred years' release.

After learning of several hand loom weavers who were still alive, and one who was still weaving, we determined to interview some of them. In the event we only interviewed two – the weavers still have a very close community and are reluctant to disclose the secrets of their trade, even though there are few of them left. The still active weaver (at Cartwright and Sheldon, a mill in Macclesfield) was Mr. James Clarke, who happened to be a next-door neighbour of one of the researchers working on this project. This interview was thus easily obtained and proved to be fruitful. Mr. Jo Brown was met through a personal contact with an interest in local history. Both being in their late sixties we realized the danger of intimidating them with a barrage of questions. We therefore constructed a series of questions which we hoped would promote discussion without the atmosphere of an interrogation; but we did feel that an outline plan of the discussion to be conducted was essential if we were to avoid being side-tracked into irrelevance. It is advisable to explain before the interview exactly what the aim of the project is. The information is too great to be solely remembered and so must be recorded on paper at the time. The use of a tape recorder was considered and would have had the advantage of perfect accuracy, but it was thought that the machine would be discomfiting to the interviewee and perhaps even to the interviewer. If conducted properly these interviews can be fruitful and enjoyable.

Interview with Mr. James (Ticker) Clarke

We first came into contact with Mr. Clarke as he is a neighbour of one of our fellow researchers, so naturally it was the neighbour who conducted the interview. He made an appointment to see him and began to prepare for the event.

We set down on paper a list of the points to jog the memory during the interview, collected together under headings such as personal, background, household, food, education, work as a weaver and life in Macclesfield. It was important to ensure that the interview did not degenerate into a series of short staccato questions and answers and the interviewer tried to keep the conversation flowing naturally, only directing its course occasionally.

We learned that Mr. Clarke was born in 1911 into a typical working class background in Macclesfield. He, his three brothers, three sisters and parents lived in a two up and two down cottage which was without a garden or bath. The house was heated by a coal fire, and all cooking was done on the range whereas gas was used for lighting. Usually there were four meals each day, the last consisting of a chip shop supper – while for Sunday lunch it was a treat to have a roast, as most other hot meals were potato hash.

He attended the local Athey Street school, leaving at 14 with no formal qualifications. It was through his father, who was a dyer, that he gained his apprenticeship as a silk weaver at Smales's Mill, which lasted for five years. He worked 10 hours a day for five days a week and Saturday mornings, with only one hour for lunch. His wages were as follows:

1st year 18/–
2nd year 23/–
3rd year 30/–
4th year Piecework
5th year Piecework

In 1931 at the age of 20 he was an accomplished weaver, making ties at the same factory, taking home £3 per week. In 1936 the depression forced him to change factories due to a shortage of work. At the onset of war in 1939 he was conscripted into the army, being de-mobbed in 1945. He then went on to work at a local textile factory, changing once again in 1950 to work for Cartwright and Sheldon, where he worked along with fifty other silkweavers. He still works there and is now the last practising hand loom silk weaver in the town.

SILK DYERS.

Barnets Messrs. Chester road
Gould Rowland, Parsonage green
Hobson Margaret and Sons, Dams
Pyatt George, (printer,) King Edward street
Smallwood Thomas & Sons, Waters Green
Smith J. and W. (printers,) Langley.
Smith Thomas, Pickford st.
Walmsley James, Green st.

SILK WEAVERS,
Who have Looms at their own Houses.

Adamson William, Richmond Hill
Adamson Patrick, Wellington street
Adshead John, Hurdsfield st.
Agnue James, Roe street
Bailey Samuel, Temple bar street
Bainbrick Pearce, Paradise street
Ball Samuel, Bank Top
Ball John, Langley
Bamford Joseph, Harberhay street
Bar Robert, Cotton street
Barber George, Bank Top
Barber Thomas, 6, Statham street
Barker Daniel, Park lane
Barlow John, Chestergate
Barlow Samuel, Hurdsfield
Barlow John, Hurdsfield
Barnes Joseph, Harberhay street
Barrington John, Mount Pleasant
Bay Abraham, Water coats
Bay John, Bank Top
Bayley Thomas, St. George street
Bayley Thomas, Cotton street

Fig.47 *An extract from a Street Directory of 1925*

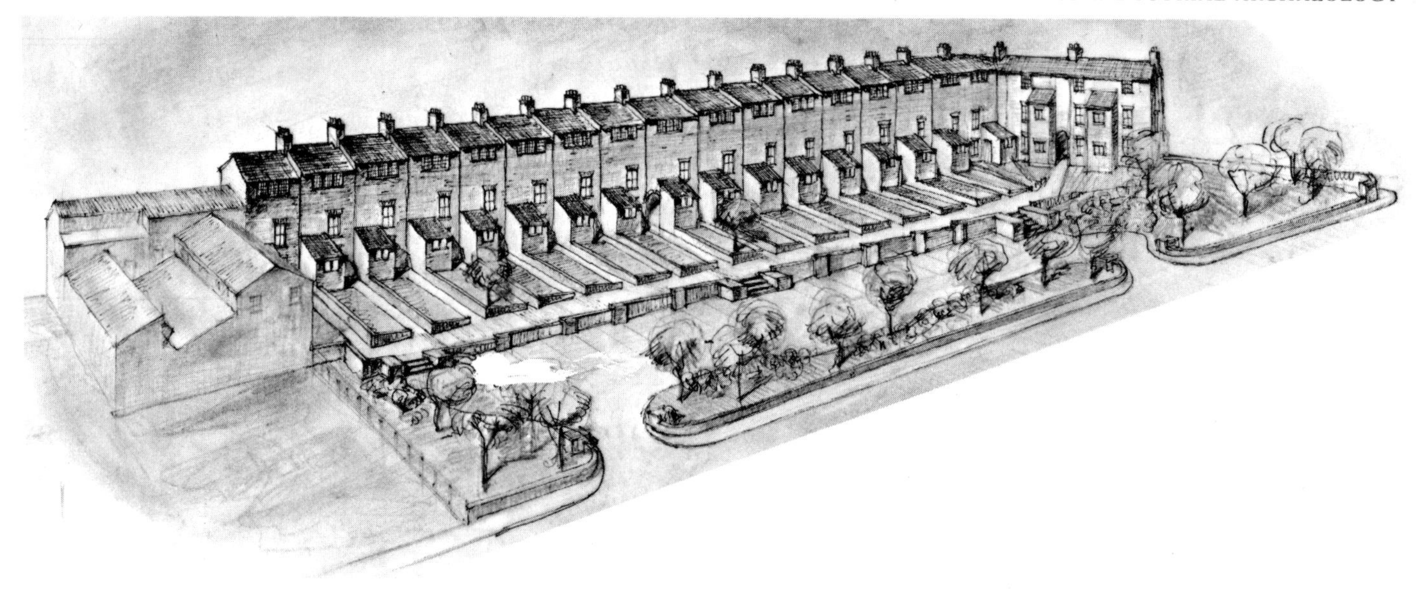

Fig.48 *Nineteen houses in Paradise Street, Macclesfield, have been modernised inside, but, as this architect's drawing shows, the exteriors have been kept exactly as they were when the houses were built.*

Fig.49 *Compare this with the back of 73 Paradise Street. Photographed in 1978 (opposite).*

As an apprentice he joined the silk weavers' union, paying 7d. a month subscription; this was later increased to 1/2d. as he qualified as a craftsman. The working conditions were fair although smoking was forbidden, and the management were hardly ever seen.

He was married in 1934 on £5 which they had saved and his first child was born in 1937. When there was a lull in orders for the silk trade he was placed on social security from which he received 15/– for the husband, 5/– for the wife and 2/– for each child, along with charity vouchers if needed.

The annual holiday was spent each year at a Blackpool boarding house to which they had to take their own food, enough to last one week.

Interview with Mr. Jo Brown

Mr. Jo Brown was born in 1911 into a working class family of five children. His mother was a weaver and his father was either unemployed or in the army; and so after a primary education at Athey Street school and having failed to win a scholarship to the King's School (the local Grammar school at Macclesfield) he was sent out to work at the age of 13. His father helped him to obtain an appointment as an Overlooker's apprentice. His duties were to tour the town to supply the silk for the looms which were in the weavers' own homes. He walked the town carrying a tray of coloured silks on small bobbins following the tackler, and it was on his first day that he received one shilling for his labour, which was a good day's work for his age.

Once having served a full seven years' apprenticeship he was able to begin work as a true craftsman and as most garrets had one or two looms in them, it took nearly half a day to fit up the looms in each house. During the week the hours of work were from 8.00 a.m. to 6.00 p.m. with an hour for lunch, but he also had to work on Saturday mornings bringing home an average wage of 14/– per week. He had eight days' holiday per year which was unpaid, and during the summer he spent a week at Blackpool and has done for the last fifty years.

After the second world war he continued in the same profession, only now his work was carried out inside a mill with 70 hand loom weavers, over which he had complete authority. It was a well paid and respected profession.

He remained in this occupation until the decline in the national and international demand for hand woven silk products forced his retirement. We were only able to obtain these facts and this information a few weeks before his death and without it, part of our industrial history would have been lost for ever.

Things to remember

Anything you find out today may be history tomorrow. So make sure that you don't lose your notes.

Make your work available to others by sending a copy of your work to the local library or Record Office.

Remember, when you are writing things down, that the person who may read them in the future may know nothing of what you are describing, so put in all the details and descriptions.

If you interview someone be sure to put down exactly who it was and why they knew the information they gave you.

An effort is being made to compile a card index of all industrial monuments from large factory buildings to small bridges or even milestones. If you find anything interesting write to the Survey Officer, the Industrial Monuments Survey, the University of Bath, Claverton Down, Bath and ask for some of their report cards. They are easy to fill in. When you send them back you will be helping to add to the store of knowledge about our industrial past.

Remember to label all photographs.

Photographs or drawings often tell more than the written word.

Tape recordings can give personality to industrial archaeology.

Keep all your notes in a book – not on scraps of paper which can get lost.

Meet other industrial archaeologists by joining your local society. If you can't find out about it write to the Association for Industrial Archaeology at Ironbridge and they will tell you about your local group. But try the local library first. A local Society may be involved in a major project, or you may find a friend there who would help with your project, or meet people interested in the same subjects.

Fig.50 *This photograph was taken many years ago by a very keen photographer. He took hundreds of pictures but died without labelling them.*

Book list

General books

The BP Book of Industrial Archaeology. Neil Cossons. (David & Charles)
Remains of a Revolution. Anthony Burton. (André Deutsch)
The Archaeology of the Industrial Revolution. Brian Bracegirdle. (Heinemann)
Discovering Industrial Archaeology and History. Hugh Bodey. (Shire Publications)

Individual subjects

So many books on different aspects of industrial archaeology have been published that it is impossible to list them all, but the subject index at your local library will give you the titles of books on any individual topic. A. & C. Black's *Industrial Archaeology Series* by Christine Vialls provides a useful introduction. The individual titles are:

Windmills and Watermills
Roads
Cast Iron
Crossing the River
Canals
Railways

Shire Publications have produced many inexpensive booklets on a wide variety of subjects.

Regional books

There are two main series of books on the industrial archaeology of individual regions, published by David & Charles and Batsford. This list includes an example from each.

The Industrial Archaeology of Cornwall. Cecil Todd and Peter Laws. (David & Charles)

The Industrial Archaeology of Scotland, the Lowlands and Borders. John R. Hume (Batsford)

Coalbrookdale and the Iron Revolution. Christine Vialls. (Cambridge University Press – from *The Cambridge Introduction to the History of Mankind*)

Biographies

Thomas Newcomen. (David & Charles)
I. K. Brunel. (Longmans)
George and Robert Stephenson. (Longmans)
James Watt. (Batsford)

all by L. T. C. Rolt

Index